DREAM THEMES

How Being Intentional with a Common Focus Can Lead to an Enhanced School Climate

WRITTEN BY ROBERT HINCHLIFFE

Self-published by Robert Hnchliffe

Las Vegas, Nevada

educationaldreamthemes@gmail.com

ISBN 9798862835625

First Printing: December 2023

DEDICATION

This book is dedicated to all the people I've worked with who have bought in to make our school climate a better place for all staff members.

TABLE OF CONTENTS

IN THE BEGINNING 1

CHOOSE YOUR PATH 6

DREAM THEME 1: THE EXTRA DEGREE 10

DREAM THEME 2: THE POWER OF ONE 13

DREAM THEME 3: R4I5E (RAISE) THE BAR 17

DREAM THEME 4: PATIENCE 20

DREAM THEME 5: WHAT IS YOUR WHY? 23

DREAM THEME 6: MOVE YOUR BUS 29

DREAM THEME 7: AWESOME AIN'T EASY 34

DREAM THEME 8: ROW THE BOAT 38

DREAM THEME 9: THE WILD CARD 44

DREAM THEME 10: BE RELENTLESS 49

DREAM THEME 11: RELATIONSHIPS OVER EVERYTHING 54

DREAM THEME 12: #LIVEYOURPURPOSE 60

DREAM THEME 13: TED TALKS 67

DREAM THEME 14: #100 POSITIVES 72

IN THE END...80

WORKS CITED...84

ABOUT THE AUTHOR 85

IN THE BEGINNING

"I just wish that people would understand that relationships matter more than anything else!"

Statements like that from teachers can happen at any time and can change the direction of your path. What you think may be your course can quickly take a turn that you didn't see coming which will help lead to the place you want to go.

In today's world, people want to be inspired! They need to have purpose. They want to be led and to lead, as well as to be recognized for their work and actions. Those same people set the tone and give a school building a feeling of joy and success. My friend and co-author of the book, *Building Dynamic Teams in Schools*, Dr. Brad

Johnson often states on social media that he can tell what the climate is of a school the moment he walks in the front door.

When schools have themes, they can be rallying points when they are done right. A leader can take a statement like the one above and utilize it for a bigger outcome. They themselves also have the potential to boost morale and create a culture of success in an area that will help move the climate in a positive way. The potential joy and outcomes are really endless when you have a North Star, a frame of reference, a common bond to strive toward.

When the Vegas Golden Knights were born in 2017 and the players were selected in the expansion draft, they were labeled "The Misfits" because essentially, they were a bunch of individuals that were cast offs, or people that didn't "fit" into an organization. The "Misfits" gelled into a formidable team who made it to the Stanley Cup Finals that first year. Six years later, their "theme" or "mantra" was, "It hurts to win." I am guessing all the pain went away as they hoisted the Stanley Cup trophy in June of 2023.

When people have these "mantras" to push them in directions, they can do great things. The statements provide inspiration because there are countless examples of famous people or actions that can be a catalyst to making a person or team see how they can be better as individuals or groups of people. However, it takes more than just introducing a statement like, "it hurts to win" to create buy-in with a theme. You need to provide positive examples and ways to reward the actions that revolve around them.

Mark Perma summarized themes or rally points as "the common ground an organization stands on, the one destination that everyone in the organization wants to reach. A powerful rally point brings people together—even people with different priorities and agendas—in support of a common goal."

Themes and rallying points are not mission statements. Mission statements tend to be written on a wall and never looked at again in schools. The common idea that, "we believe that all children can lead and be lifelong learners as well as great humans" should automatically be part of your culture, but a theme that builds a school has many features other than this.

First off, it has to be relevant to what you are trying to accomplish as a staff this year or at that moment. Not ten years from now. It is a point in time that you want to get to which will lead your organization to the ultimate goal. If your dream is to have a culture where everyone works together, you have to take steps to reach that point eventually.

All schools want all students to grow and for every student to be proficient on exams. Every organization wants to be at the top of their field. All teams want to win a championship. But there are steps to this process, and they rarely happen just by starting.

At times, the circumstances that surround you will lead you to your first step. In the show *Ted Lasso*, the first item to tackle was to create a team that had a group of people who were all in for each other. Ted didn't believe in measuring success by wins or losses, rather if the team was just that, a team. He also needed them to "believe" in the team and his process. The sign that hung above the door was a reminder, as well as the activities that they did. It wasn't as much about practice as it was about bringing people together because without that, the group wouldn't be able to achieve greatness, which was the ultimate goal. In the end, that baby step of creating relationships was the catalyst to a turnaround which led to extreme success.

At Tyrone Thompson Elementary School, we were tasked with the monumental challenge of opening a brand-new school ONLINE in September of 2020 during the Covid-19 pandemic. While yes, the goal was for kids to continue to learn and we wanted to keep them as proficient as they were or still grow them, to say our "theme" was "success for all" wouldn't have been poignant at that time. We could have said, "come together and help everyone" but that didn't work either given the circumstances. That year, we used the book, *The Wild Card* as a rallying point. Hope and Wade King's book does a fabulous job of explaining why the people on campus, especially the teachers, are "the wild card" in the hands that you were dealt. We were, in essence, given the hand of opening a school at that point in time in the world and we had to succeed. The theme, discussed more in a later chapter, essentially stated that we were in control of our destiny that year and we had to be the people to find a way to make learning happen.

Rallying points give a team a purpose. A target. A place to center the group so that we can all grow together for a common good. They get people ready for a year and bring them back to the center when they get off course at times. It allows others to see the good deeds of others within this framework as well. They also evolve over time, as you will see in the examples that follow and grow as you implement them into the fabric of your school. But what is a good theme? How do you find this rallying point? Should the mantra apply to all people or just some? Let's examine these thoughts.

CHOOSE YOUR PATH

Any school can create a theme, but to live it is an entirely different thing. One can say, "We are going to grow" and basically then it is left alone after the first day. Or someone may say, "Happy Days with Happy Ways" and preach about being full of smiles and joy, yet after people get into the trenches, the smiles and joys aren't celebrated.

You must be all in with a theme, otherwise it is just a statement. Anyone can say anything that sounds good, but to live and breathe it requires thought and effort, which is where many people fall short.

When you think of something that is "big picture" that you want to work on for your staff or organization, you need it to be catchy. Something people can get excited about! It could be short as well. You shouldn't have something like

#wegonnarockandourkidswillsucceedinmath. Nobody is going to say that when they are passing by each other in the halls.

Theme titles must be short, and more importantly, relevant! Nearly any statement can be made to fit into the square, but how it is sold should bring it back to the goal of what you are trying to accomplish. A place cannot say "#1 in all things" when you aren't #1 in anything. The mantra must be attainable, but here is the next part, mentally measurable.

When I say "mentally measurable" the key word is mentally. You do not necessarily need something you can quantify, rather, something people can take and ask themselves, "*did I do that this year based upon the criteria set forth?*" For example, if your theme is "Be Relentless" (which we will discuss later as well), can you quantify that or is it something that one can answer with an example that maybe nobody knows about? Was a person relentlessly working to change a student's behavior or positively correcting a child each day to create excellent habits? How can one be honest with themselves and answer the question, "*did I accomplish the theme in some way this year?*"

Themes need examples as well. The person who is revealing the theme must point people in the right direction. For example, if we are rallying around the idea of relationships, we would want to point to positive ways that relationships have changed students' trajectories or perhaps, as *Ted Lasso* modeled, when people have relationships with their teammates, the team is the winner.

Think of the pitfalls of what you are saying and determine if the pros outweigh the cons. Are there nuances that can lead to negativity? Again, going back to the example "#1 in all things", this can also lend itself to being #1 in dropouts, chronic absenteeism, suspensions, and other negative outcomes.

Finally, it has shelf life. Sadly, most principals or leaders start to lose their ability to connect with the staff around seven years into the job. Things don't resonate and hearing the same peppy stuff from the same person each year can be tiring. Themes have a shelf life of a year, maybe two. You can tie the old ones in (explained in the chapter on #liveyourpurpose) and have them build on top of each other, but to use the same one gets redundant and loses its connectivity with the group quickly.

Once you have picked your theme based upon the above criteria, now you have to set it up for success. This is where the real work begins! How will you reveal it? Who/what will help people be inspired to live it and "buy in" to the idea? How are you going to reward/recognize individual acts that pertain to what the overall vision of the goal is? Is there an even bigger celebration that can inspire, motivate, and give examples to those who maybe struggle with making this mantra a part of their lives? Are we going to design shirts for the staff that go with this theme? How can you pull people in to help you with this theme, so it is even more powerful? Do we include the school community also and work to get "buy in" from every stakeholder?

As we begin to look at ideas, ultimately, you must make them yours! Copying may work, but I should point you back to the "relevant" part. Yes, some of the examples may fit at the right time for you, and you may run with them, but don't be status quo and do the average. Personalize things and get more "buy in" to rally the people you wish to inspire!

The themes that you are about to read show a maturation of the idea, starting from a very basic idea that worked to get people to go the extra mile. By the end, you see how the idea of yearly themes has taken on a life of its own. A simple idea has grown over the years into something that is celebrated by staff when it is revealed because it gives them a bit more of a motivational edge for the year. You are about to take a journey through the years and see how it has blossomed, and, at the end, I hope that you will be inspired to create a "dream theme" that brings out the same passion in a team as it does for the school that I lead on a daily basis.

DREAM THEME 1: THE EXTRA DEGREE

"At 211* water is hot. At 212' it boils, and with boiling water comes steam...and with steam, you can power a train."

S.L Parker

I first had a snippet of a theme that was used when I was in my sixth year as an Assistant Principal in Las Vegas. The principal at the time gave me a book to welcome me to the school called "212 the Extra Degree" which she used a bit to inspire the people. I learned that there is a whole set of materials online that apply to this concept, including little cards for people when they go to the extra degree. People would then place these cards on a bulletin board to recognize someone who went above and beyond in some way.

My first year as a principal, I took this idea to " The Extra Degree" and began the journey of themes. At the first meeting when I was introduced to the entire staff as they came back from summer break, I played a video that essentially had the book text within a movie. From there, I decided to recognize three people who had already gone the extra degree with what I called a "212" award. I made a certificate and purchased plaques that could be put together yet exuded high quality and gave a very specific statement about why each had gone the extra degree prior to handing them a plaque. The idea of "212" was cemented in everyone's minds and from then on, any time I gave a "212" award, they knew what that entailed. I also hung a small bulletin board just outside my office and introduced the idea of "212 cards" which caught on, there even further put their names on the "Friday Forecast" to ensure that everyone saw who was going above and beyond.

DREAM THEME # 1: THE EXTRA DEGREE

EASE OF IMPLEMENTATION: This theme is easily accomplished. Much of what you need is online or can be created.

RELEVANCE: All people should be attempting to go above and beyond (aka the extra degree) in their profession each and every day. With education, this can take on many forms. If the administration wanted to dial it in and say "212 in the area of math" and then highlight excellence in that area, that would work. There are a multitude of ways to make this relevant in any organization.

MENTAL MEASURABILITY: Yes! Everyone can look in the mirror and ask if they were a "212" or if they went the extra degree. Others can see or hear about the actions taken by colleagues and measure it.

EXAMPLES: They are everywhere! Google "famous people who went above and beyond" and then have one that applies to your situation. Use this person as a way to connect to your staff to maximize intrinsic impact and motivation.

PITFALLS: One person's "212" is another person's "157" degrees. Not everyone will agree with what deserves recognition. Others may write a "212" just because their friend showed up to work. Reward positive examples and work to hone in the criteria of the acts that will move the organization forward in the direction you want.

THE REVEAL: It is all done for you. Show the video that goes along with the quote above. Then reward huge behaviors that everyone can get behind. From there, continue to build it up. Wanna get crazy? Dress up like a conductor, rent a bus, and go take the staff on a train ride prior to showing the movie. Better yet, read the book on the train while they drink some "hot" chocolate.

WHO / WHAT WILL GET BUY-IN TO THE IDEA? The principal or leader sets the tone, so how you want to get "buy in" is up to you, but use examples and reward the right people in your organization or you'll fall flat. Be strategic and use it to recognize someone who needs that boost to get going. Timing and relevance are huge!

OTHER STAKEHOLDERS: Have parents write 212 cards as well!

DREAM THEME 2: THE POWER OF ONE

I noticed an area of need during my first year of supervising my school that led me to the next theme. Many times, we were just using lower-level questioning and surface level answers were abundant. Assessments at the time were continuing to get more complex and we needed to move in the direction of challenging students at a deeper level of understanding. Our academic vocabulary was also not prevalent in many rooms which was leading students to have difficulty explaining answers.

How was I going to get the point across to the staff? I was going to immerse them in words that mattered. The clerk at our school had the ability to cut vinyl, which was rare back in 2013, yet it was a huge advantage to me with this process. I wrote down as many higher order "Bloom's Taxonomy" verbs as I can find that fit elementary school and added it to the list of basic vocabulary words that students needed in order to succeed. Words like "sum, difference, factor, multiple" and on and on. The clerk, bless her heart, cut probably 100 words in black vinyl and handed them over. From there, each was strategically placed throughout campus.

In the primary area were more primary words, and on the other side of the building were words that aligned to the standards in grades 3-5. The school's library was in the middle of the building, so it was littered with terms like "fiction and nonfiction" so that students would hopefully get their understanding both through the lesson and osmosis.

To kick this idea off, the staff obviously saw the words when they returned from summer break, but I threw in a personal story about it. That same summer I was enjoying my family, and the girls were very young (6 and 3). But as I have found, it is hard to have everything perfect in your life at both work and home, so when a girlfriend at the time decided to make a change, it was hurtful. The entire conversation showed that what you say is important and words matter to people. "The Power of ONE" word can change the entire direction of your thoughts and life. Love, pain, anxiety, loss, joy, hope – each of these single words holds an immense amount of power, just like each word that we had placed on the walls of the building. I had to tell the staff about the life change that happened to me, so why not use it to my advantage with the theme and evoke some emotions! The story struck home, as everyone can think of a time that somebody said something that hurt them, and when you combined it with the words around the school, they got the significance of what I was trying to accomplish with vocabulary.

This is the first time that I realized that being vulnerable and sharing part of your life helps you connect with those that you work with, even when you are the "boss" technically. They want to know who you are and have a relationship with you, not just know you as someone who is driving the bus. Use personal stories to connect the dots, and they will use their own personal stories to then internalize themes which motivates and encourages "buy in".

DREAM THEME # 2: THE POWER OF ONE

EASE OF IMPLEMENTATION: Medium. Vinyl takes time and effort to cut and hang, assuming you have someone who can do it.

RELEVANCE: High! Words always matter, especially in 2024! We have to be sensitive to all people, yet we must use academic vocabulary on a daily basis to ensure students can explain their work appropriately.

MENTAL MEASURABILITY: Yes! All staff can think, "Did I use a higher order word? Did I use the right words when working with kids?"

EXAMPLES: There are so many individuals being called out for using incorrect words in today's world that a simple google search can lead to plenty of examples. Right or wrong, there are stories everywhere that prove "words matter", but the best example would be a personal experience that can be shared.

PITFALLS: People are sensitive to a lot. Your story or words may cause trauma or pain. Keep others in mind as you plot this out.

THE REVEAL: It is hard to hide words that now adorn your building. However, the people returning could have fun with it. Perhaps have them do a puzzle with some of them, or maybe they have to run around the building and use a certain group of words in a story about why "words matter" to them. Have some fun!

WHO / WHAT WILL GET BUY-IN TO THE IDEA? Make it personal! Emotions are the best motivator!

DREAM THEME 3: R415E (RAISE) THE BAR

In my younger days, I used to run a lot more than I do now. And as I implied at the very first part of the book: you never know when a phrase or action will cause your path to turn.

Heading into my 3rd year as principal, I wanted to keep the momentum rolling with themes. We had a good first and second year and I had a grasp on the school and community, as well as the staff members, but I was looking for more! We were doing well, but since I believe that every organization wants to finish 1st and that 2nd place is the first loser, we needed to keep going. However, I couldn't find something that fit. I had tried a few ideas out mentally, but they just didn't feel right, until one day it happened.

In Las Vegas, every school has a location code, and the school I was at was #415. I happened to be running at the gym on a treadmill and I looked up to see someone in front of me with a shirt that said, "Raise the bar" and it was of a person working out with a barbell. The odd thing was that the "AIS" in the word "raise" legitimately was the school number 415. It was just meant to be! And that was our mantra for the year.

Where I "dropped the bar" so to speak was the reveal. I had a PowerPoint and within it was some data and then I had a fancy way to make the "AIS" turn into "415" and show how it works. The only problem was that very few people knew our school was "415" because teachers do not use the code that often!

At any rate, that is where the "relevance" comes in. Even if we were not "415", you can still use "raise the bar" and have a fun time doing that. There isn't ever a bad time to raise scores or outcomes in a positive way in your school.

DREAM THEME # 3: RAISE (RAISE) THE BAR

EASE OF IMPLEMENTATION: Simple! This one was easy, it just missed the mark and taught me to be better with everything. If you have a number that can connect with your school, that is great! Maybe it is the number in your street address, but using a number to create a theme is easy if you have one that works. Looking back on it, I would have found a different way to wrap in the relevance. Raising the bar is a great idea, but the number has to have a connection.

RELEVANCE: Everyone can raise their output and standards of excellence. This can be applied personally or professionally in simple to complex ways.

MENTAL MEASURABILITY: Yes! Did you "raise the bar" with your outcomes, whichever they may be?

EXAMPLES: Use sports examples or examples of schools who were able to raise test scores. There are tons of examples of people growing in many areas. For a real world example, bring in the story of Dick Fosbury and explain how he had to "raise the bar" because he invented a new way of high jumping in the Olympics and set new records in doing so.

PITFALLS: You don't want to raise the wrong items, such as truancy, parent complaints, or vacancies. But if you can keep it positive, then raise it up!

THE REVEAL: Have a personal trainer come in and provide some examples of exercises that require a bar. Perhaps meet at a gym or utilize the equipment outside and create an activity that is fun. What about a limbo, but then turn it around because we don't want people lowering the bar!

WHO / WHAT WILL GET BUY-IN TO THE IDEA? You have to find a connection somehow! If your people enjoy fitness, this will be right up their alley. Partner with a gym for free memberships or for them to provide healthy snacks for the lounge so that people are reminded to raise the bar. Throw in some "raisins" often or create some fun ideas with that snack!

DREAM THEME 4: PATIENCE

"All we need is just a little patience."

Axl Rose - Patience

My 3rd year as principal brought on many changes. Our district was moving toward a new program that had all student information, grades, and various other features as we were gradually beginning to move away from all forms of paper. We were also getting more and more into other technologies and the school that I was at needed this change to occur because we were antiquated in so many ways. That being said, it was a lot, essentially for a group of teachers who already were doing "212" type things and also why they were trying to "R415e the bar" in other areas. To compound the changes, we were welcoming six new staff members to the school, which was a large amount for a place that was historically stable. As I looked around, I could see some angst with the amount of change that they were about to endure. But I knew if we could work together and stay "patient" that this group could handle it.

Enter Axl Rose. Not more than a few minutes into the opening meeting, I stopped and turned on the song by Guns and Roses. As Axl Rose opens up with the famous whistling in the song, I took off my shirt that was over another tee shirt that had no sleeves, then tied a bandana around my head. The only thing missing were the tattoos and the leather pants!

It was a hoot, and it got their attention. Next, on the screen, I clicked through each "change" and explained how it would affect us, then said "Patience" but also, they had to whistle the main part of the opening but every time they heard it. Imagine that. A guy dressed like the lead singer of a band from the 80s had the staff whistle at every change that was coming our way. Funny to think about now, but it got the point across that we had to be "Patient" and stick together and not get upset with our colleagues. People take on change better than others and the last thing I wanted was to have to create animosity or issues in the school. Overall, they were patient, and I don't remember anything traumatic happening because of all the upgrades, so the theme kept them focused on the broader goal of getting better with the new tools and colleagues that were now a part of the building.

DREAM THEME # 4: PATIENCE

EASE OF IMPLEMENTATION: Are you willing to dress up and do you like Guns and Roses? If so, it's fairly easy! The "experienced" individuals may know who Axl Rose is, however, many will not. I would put on the video of the song in some way prior for some background knowledge if I were to do it these days. Remember, if they cannot connect to the message and the examples, the moment may be lost.

RELEVANCE: Depends on your current circumstances. Do you need them to be patient? In today's world, with all of the new programs and items being thrown at teachers, patience and understanding could be huge. If you were starting a new school, you may hope that everyone just takes a breath as you figure out the way the school is going to run while ironing out any issues that arise during that first few years. Themes need to be relevant and meaningful, as implied often, for them to be purposeful.

MENTAL MEASURABILITY: Yes! They know if they have lost their "patience" or not. Every educator does at some point in the year, but if they can keep their cool more than usual in the face of changes, they can say they accomplished the goal.

EXAMPLES: See above

PITFALLS: It has to be the right time. It could be a hard theme to use in education because right now we have more urgency than any other time. Also, "Guns" and schools rarely mix well. Following along, the message of why to be patient would need to be very clear. You do not want a teacher who is struggling to start whistling "Patience" or someone to invoke Axl Rose when their outcomes are lagging behind the pack.

THE REVEAL: Perhaps you know Axl Rose or someone who sings? A band that can cover GNR? Maybe you all plant roses and watch them grow throughout the year. Have everyone bring in a sleeveless white T-shirt and they can write "patience" on it. Just make sure the song is there! :)

WHO / WHAT WILL GET BUY-IN TO THE IDEA? 80s rock fans are in! Send the staff roses from a flower shop. Have parents send in roses from time to time. Have the beginning of the song open up every meeting and wait until most are trying to whistle along with the tune. It could be a call back. The leader of the meeting could say, "All we need is," and the participants say, "just a little patience!"

DREAM THEME 5: WHAT IS YOUR WHY?

I was at a conference in Phoenix with some teacher leaders one year. It was a Solution Tree event, and the keynote speaker was Mike Mattos. He was describing how his staff had enjoyed great success when he uttered the words, "know your why!" The year was 2016 and the idea behind a "why" movement really was just getting started. However, that was another one of those moments where the course of the year took on a different meaning. Little did I know that it would become more prevalent a few months later.

In March of 2016, I began to experience symptoms that no person wants to have, and it was discovered not long after that I had a tumor that needed to be removed. It was operable, but the road to recovery was difficult, and that was after chemo and radiation. The entire summer I had to overcome those obstacles while thinking about my fate all while planning for another school year. The tasks that were needing to be completed helped get me from day to day and kept my mind off of mortality, but my "why" was pretty clear during this time. Having a family and knowing that five daughters needed me can be pretty motivating. But, as I said before in the chapter "words matter", I believe that using personal stories and experiences to evoke emotion is a great way to hook the staff and get "buy in" to what you are trying to accomplish.

In the days leading up to the grand reveal of "What is Your Why?" I had people notice my chemo pack (I was able to wear a machine that delivered the chemo outside of the hospital during the week), yet only one person asked what it was. I simply said, "you'll find out Wednesday" (the day staff returned).

Along with Mike Mattos and my cancer, a movie titled, *Gleason* was released into theaters.

Gleason tells the story of Steve Gleason, a former NFL player who is credited with starting what is called the "rebirth" in New Orleans a year after Hurricane Katrina decimated the city. That is really just the beginning of the story from my perspective though.

Steve Gleason was born 12 days before me on March 19, 1977. He grew up in Spokane, Washington, which is 120 miles or so from my hometown of Waitsburg. Amazingly enough, I heard his name numerous times on television on Friday nights as he became a football star at his high school. In the early to mid-1990s we didn't have the internet, so we tuned into the news out of Spokane to see our football scores on the television and that is how we found out if the teams in other leagues won or lost. It was either that or we had to wait to read it in the Sunday morning paper. Often, and because the stations tended to give the teams from Spokane more airtime and show highlights, Gonzaga Prep would be featured, and I would hear that name on occasion. Over the course of a few years, I heard it on more than a few occasions.

In 1995 after high school graduation, I headed off to the University of Idaho in Moscow to pursue a teaching degree. I received a decent scholarship to attend there, but my heart was always with the Cougars of Washington State in Pullman, eight miles away.

Attending the Cougar games was standard on the Saturdays they played at home in Martin Stadium, and it wasn't too long before a familiar name started to get announced for making tackles. Steve Gleason was growing into an outstanding college football player. It was only natural for me to follow his career and even more enjoyable to see an undersized linebacker find his way onto an NFL team as a special teams player. Being from a small town and having watched him from afar as we grew up, it was neat to view his journey which eventually led him to the New Orleans Saints. It was here that the legend began, and where it continues today.

In the first game back at the Superdome, the crowd was in full force to see their Saints and get some normalcy back. In the first series, the Falcons went three and out thus having to punt the ball. And it is then that a guy I had followed from our youth spring into immortality. Steve Gleason blocked the punt and the Saints scored, sending the stadium into a frenzy and triggering the "rebirth" of New Orleans.

The movie *Gleason* highlights the blocked punt, but what people don't know is that a few years later, Steve Gleason was diagnosed with ALS (Lou Gehrig's disease) and his life was completely altered. The powerful movie shows the stages of deterioration of his body and abilities while encapsulating his growth mindset as he faces the facts that the illness brings. It is a movie that makes you grateful for the things you have in life.

For the reveal, I began with a quick little talk about a pilot and how they have to file their flight plan. Everyone was to draw their route over the months of a calendar (think of a grid with each line as a month), but I had them do a dip in the month of December and label it "turbulence". I then told them that this is the month I would be out because I was having surgery to remove the growth that was in my body. Boom. I had them. Many were shocked, a few tears were shed. Some had a question or two that I answered. But then, I played the trailer of the movie *Gleason* (more tears!) and at the end said, my problems are tiny compared to his. He has a disease that is taking everything from him except his eyesight and his ability to think and see it all happen to him. I just have to have chemo, radiation, surgery and recover. That, my friends, brings perspective. I then told everyone about Mike Mattos and "your why" and said that professionally they were my "why" and the reason I was there instead of on family medical leave. We had a job to do, and I was going to help my "why" get it done. I then gave them a vinyl sticker (yes, more vinyl!) that said, "What is YOUR why?" so that they could put it somewhere in their room to remind them of why they are at work doing the job they do.

Powerful. And as for Steve Gleason, he has had a bigger impact as a human after his diagnosis than as the guy who blocked the punt. Ice bucket challenge, anyone?

DREAM THEME # 5: WHAT IS YOUR WHY?

EASE OF IMPLEMENTATION: Simple. Just find your backstory.

RELEVANCE: Everyone has their why. You just gotta tap into their emotions and make them remember it and "why" they do what they do.

MENTAL MEASURABILITY: Yes! We have a built-in reminder of why we do the things we do and who we do them for. Are you remembering your "why" right now?

EXAMPLES: Hardships happen to many. You can use Steve Gleason as an example.

PITFALLS: Minimal

THE REVEAL: Get creative. Sure you can make a "what is your why?" sticker, but bring it to the forefront. Maybe have them write a heartfelt letter to the person who is the "why" behind them being where they are at. Play a video of Mr. Rogers where he implored people to thank the ones who made an impact in their lives. There are many ways to bring a person's "why" to the front of their mind.

WHO / WHAT WILL GET BUY-IN TO THE IDEA? Emotions. Tug on the heart strings. Have cards that staff can fill out and send to each other telling them "why" they are doing amazing for kids. Then have parents or kids say "why" they are important to them every day.

DREAM THEME 6: MOVE YOUR BUS

There is a great video by Ron Clark, of the world-famous Ron Clark Academy in Atlanta, Georgia, where he talks about the members of his (or any) organization. While being a fantastic storyteller, he gives definitions of the four types of individuals within his school. Explained in much more depth through the chapters of his book, *Move Your Bus*, it is a fantastic way to build some momentum in your school, motivate your "runners" and push your "riders" out the door.

Every business and school has a person or multiple that just needs to go. Sometimes it is the boss, but that's a different book! We all have teachers or support staff that have overstayed their welcome, yet will not reflect enough to make a great personal and professional decision for themselves. My school was and is no different at points in time.

Using books written by extremely motivating or famous people can become one of the best themes you can create because everyone can find something to connect to within the texts and chapters. In the case of "Move Your Bus", my goal was to keep the "runners" running and have people reflect on if they were riding and needed to get off at the next stop. Moving a school forward as an entity can only go as fast as the slowest mover, but in education, removing the riders can be more work that it is worth at times.

Some of my philosophical beliefs on working with staff members have been adopted from Mr. Clark and are based on the way he can define individuals through the characteristics of their work ethic and contributions to your group.

In March of 2018, my wife and I traveled to Atlanta to take part in the Ron Clark Experience. At the time, I didn't know what exactly I was looking for from the trip, but it didn't take long to find it. Being on the west coast in Las Vegas, traveling back east is a challenge. Being at RCA at 7:30 actually means 4:30 western time, which requires a 3:30 (at the latest) wake up call. If your plane doesn't arrive early, that can make for a tough turnaround. Yet, even with the challenge of getting up that early, I was struck quickly with an energy that I am yet to feel at any other school on a consistent basis.

On this day, hundreds of people are waiting outside the gates and then begin the journey into the building. As you walk down the sidewalk after entering, you begin hearing music and start to think, "Whoa" and that's when you turn left and enter a new realm of possibility within a school.

Imagine the music pumping, kids dancing and clapping, energy everywhere, and then you see him. Sharply dressed as only he can do, welcoming people and dancing as well. The energy is through the roof, and you can feel what it is like to be at a place where fun happens while learning content at the next level.

My mind shifted to, "*How do we do this in public school?*" And I began to take notes, but then got the low down when in Mr. Clark's room watching him teach, as well as listening to him give his perspective on the people who make a building run.

First, he had extremely high expectations for himself and his students. He taught the entire lesson without speaking and students are extremely critical of their classmates with their peer review. Second, through what I comprehended as he described runners, joggers, walkers, and riders was that ultimately it is the people who make the difference. I knew this, but sometimes you have to hear it and see it from another person.

Bringing it back to school as a theme was easy. The first day back you teach them the four types of people, then you have them mentally identify where they are and give them grace with their self-assessments. The riders know who they are, yet they aren't going to admit it openly. Walkers think they're joggers, joggers think they are runners, and runners think they are joggers and need to go faster. In the end, have people identify the areas they can run in, and then encourage them to cheer when they are riding.

Over time, I have taken this concept and now feel that everyone is a sprinter in their own area. Not all of us can run all the time, yet we all sprint in some areas. Use positive examples of the types of running you are looking for in your building, recognize great actions often, and focus on the people who are making your bus move faster. Those are the people to spend time on.

DREAM THEME # 6: MOVE YOUR BUS

EASE OF IMPLEMENTATION: Simple to challenging. Ultimately if you want people to understand RCA, you have to send them there for PD. You can show videos and define the personalities, which is fairly easy, but for the full effect, travel is a must.

RELEVANCE: We don't have time for inconsistent bus riders these days. They need off at the next stop. We also need the runners to run! It's all relevant when you look at it through the eyes of what we need at our building. We need urgency and to sprint where we can so our bus moves faster!

MENTAL MEASURABILITY: Yes! Are you riding or are you running? If people are honest with themselves, and reflect looking to improve, they will let you know where the struggle bus is located for them personally. From there, you help them get back on the right bus!

EXAMPLES: People on your staff see those that go above and beyond. It's not hard to identify them. You can also find people in life who were the runners, and plenty of clips in movies of those who slowed down the team.

PITFALLS: Minimal to some. Some people don't like being labeled, which is usually the ones hurting the speed of the team. Also, professional development can be expensive if traveling to Atlanta.

THE REVEAL: Show a clip of Ron Clark describing the members of the organization. Then, discuss them or have them run all over the building to accomplish a team building mission. In these types of activities, the people fit into the four categories. The runners are the competitive ones. The riders watch everyone do the work. Finish with a clip of Tom Hanks in Forrest Gump saying, "from that day, if I was going somewhere, I was running!" Throw in some chocolates on the table as well, because they are all different, and sometimes you never know what you're gonna get.

WHO / WHAT WILL GET BUY-IN TO THE IDEA? Emotions. Have parents write notes when someone goes above and beyond. Have "212" cards that are buses that people can give praise to those runners.

DREAM THEME 7: AWESOME AIN'T EASY

"Are you a coroner? Because pronouncing people dead is not part of our job description. We never stop, Jake. Not from the cabin to the tarmac. We never stop."

Kevin Costner as Ben Randall

This scene is from the movie *The Guardian* in 2006 which is about new recruits who are starting their training to qualify for the Coast Guard. Ashton Kutcher plays Jake, who is a hot shot with secret baggage that comes to light near the middle of the movie. Kevin Costner plays Ben Randall, the Senior Chief who has his own demons yet has been assigned to train this new group of individuals who think they want to rescue people, and he isn't too excited about the new role.

Although he isn't thrilled, he takes over and does things his way, which leads to the trainees in a pool of ice-cold water learning about hypothermia. At one point, he is questioned about his methods and told there are classrooms to teach them about that scenario to which he replies, "Sir, in about two and a half minutes they'll understand."

Continuing that lesson leads to the quotes at the start of the chapter, but especially the part where Chief Randall says, "we never give up, Jake."

When you combine this movie with the movie discussed in Chapter 5 (*Gleason*) we have some extremely poignant and powerful lessons that can be learned as well as some statements that are excellent for yearlong themes, which is where we headed after, "What is YOUR why?"

The movie ends with Steve saying, "I believe my purpose is bigger than my past." which is foreshadowing the even more amazing accomplishments of his life. After the film was released to critical acclaim, his story really took off.

In the years following, Steve Gleason has led the charge against ALS, working to fight to save people afflicted with the terrible prognosis. His foundation is called, "No White Flags" and he based that title off of his football career (penalties flags) and the white for surrendering. "No White Flags" is a metaphor for never giving up no matter what adversity one may face. Steve also works to provide opportunities for those who have been diagnosed with ALS, much like "Make A Wish" and has given many people a way to live with dignity and purpose.

During his movie, Gleason also has a phrase that he used which is, "Awesome Ain't Easy." When you think about it, there is no truer statement out there. It is hard to be awesome. It takes effort to be amazing and reach new heights of achievement. Being status quo and average is not only easy, but it is pretty much the norm these days, especially in the profession of education.

So, when we take these two movies in total and work to make a theme for a school year, there are many ways to go. Being that Steve Gleason is my adult idol as well as near and dear to me, I chose "Awesome Ain't Easy!"

At the point in time we were at with the school, we were headed in the right direction and needed to just take it up a notch. Essentially, I had a team builder activity (MAKE IT FUN!) and then had Steve Gleason on the overhead with a picture of "No White Flags" on his forearm and then everyone took a picture with a big selfie frame that help the inscription "Awesome Ain't Easy" written on it.

We then sent them the picture as a reminder to not be status quo for the year, and they weren't. The school was deemed a "Distinguished Star" and "5-star" rated school and it was thanks to them being "awesome".

DREAM THEME # 7: AWESOME AIN'T EASY

EASE OF IMPLEMENTATION: Simple.

RELEVANCE: We need schools to be more than awesome these days. The status quo is not moving the needle.

MENTAL MEASURABILITY: Yes! Did they give up on a kid? Were they awesome?

EXAMPLES: Examples of "awesome" are everywhere. Find some that apply to your school or staff and make them relevant to their lives.

PITFALLS: Minimal. Perhaps someone knows someone who is afflicted with ALS, which could be traumatizing.

THE REVEAL: Get creative. Have a montage of "awesome" things about your school, or the people around the building and tell stories about how the actions were not easy to accomplish but they made them happen. You could also get crazy and invite the Coast Guard to talk about how their "awesome ain't easy".

WHO / WHAT WILL GET BUY-IN TO THE IDEA? More emotions. Tug on the heart strings. Show them how they are awesome, how they haven't given up, or get them some "white flags" with the word "NO" on it!

DREAM THEME 8: ROW THE BOAT

"If there is no wind, row."

Chinese Proverb

In my final year at the school where the "Dream Themes" all started, the staff really needed one of my best pep talks. I was in year 8, and for all the accolades that we had received, we knew that it was going to be a down year rating-wise based off of what we projected our achievement on state assessments to be. It was a balance between positive praise, but also the need to motivate in order to overcome the adversity we were going to face.

When I was in high school, in my small hometown, it was essentially the concept that "football was life" for me. Like so many teenagers, *Friday Night Lights* was real life. During my junior year, we were in the state quarterfinals and as the quarterback, I played my part on the team to the best of my ability and gave it my all each game. In the playoff game the year before, we were beaten 46-0 by the same team we were up against, on the same field, one year later. The only difference was that this time, we were more confident and had a chance.

In the 4th quarter we were down 44-40 and, in the end, I made a huge blunder and blew the game. It was 100% my fault and there was no excuse for the fact I turned the ball over at the most crucial moment of the game.

During the interview with the newspaper reporter, at the end I said, "We have a really great shot next year with who we have coming back."

I'm not sure how I do it, but it is my style to remove things that could be useful that I see and just file them away for the right time. As leaders, we need to always have the right lever to pull at the correct time. We need a lot of items in our bag for tricks to motivate staff members when they need it or push them to keep going at times that are important. One such instance was when I happened upon a documentary about a person who was preaching for everyone to "change their best!" on the show. I filed that away and watched one episode and moved on.

When planning for the previous year, the assistant principal wanted to use that motto and roll with it, but I wanted to roll with Gleason and all that came with it. So, entering year 8, it was time to "change our best" which is a small part of the concept by P.J. Fleck.

Fleck is the head football coach at the University of Minnesota. He rose to that position with not only his knowledge of the game, but his insane amount of energy and his different approaches to recruiting and motivating players. He is an excellent example of a guy who uses "Dream Themes" to improve his program. In fact, I'd say he was one of the first to really put his ideas out there, and he used social media to promote his book and overall mantra of "Row the Boat."

The concept that you have to count on yourself and do the work to make outcomes happen is nothing new, but unless you really analyze it and make it at the forefront of your mind, few people think that independence and hard work will get you through the rough seas. Further, if you have a team where everyone has an oar, you can row faster and accomplish more.

"Row the Boat" signifies hard work with a purpose. You know where you want to go, you turn to avoid pitfalls, and if you paddle enough, you accomplish your goal to arrive at the destination you were aiming for at the beginning of your journey. Whether you are approaching a problem or working to meet a goal, no matter how you look at it, if you do not "row the boat" you won't succeed.

Opening the year that August, I had a great video of P.J. Fleck to start. He is in a press conference, and he pulls out a drawing of how he views "progress". It is a wonderful illustration of two lines. One is a normally straight-line angling upward on a trajectory showing a steep increase in outcomes. The other was a squiggly line that had ups and downs and turns yet it was going up to the same point as the other line. He then said, "the straight line is how people *think* growth happens but in reality, *this* is how we measure growth" pointing to the squiggly line. Fantastic! I then took his "squiggly line" and made two labels. One was at the top of a circle (last year) and one was at the bottom of a circle in his crazy line (now). The point was that yes, we were higher as a school the previous year, but we were still on a line of growth and improving daily.

I followed that up with the exact data that showed we had dropped, and basically said we had to "Row the Boat" now and get back to where we want to be. I also played a great scene from the movie *Tommy Boy* where he is stuck on a small sailboat without an oar and no wind, showing we were stuck and not going to move without working or help.

A few other P.J. Fleck videos later, I broke out a newspaper clipping in which they proceeded to read about the game I described above that I lost. It was my way of making it personable and sharing my own failure and highlighted how we had a great shot at doing well the next year with who we had on our team. All of this applied to the team in front of me. We didn't finish the year the way we hoped last year, but we had the talent to get back to the place we were and be even better than that.

This was the idea, and we ran even further with it. We changed the "212" cards to little oars and every month had a person receive them. The winners' names were written on them and then the oars were displayed next to two large paddles that we had hanging on a wall. It was fun taking it up a notch and revamping the cards that we used for so long.

Finally, taking it up even more, everyone who received an oar was given a key as well. The keys were randomly handed out and saved until the end of the semester. During a morning meeting prior to winter break, those who had a key could see if it would open a lock to a treasure chest full of prizes, most of which were donated by parents. The joy of the people who held the right key was obvious, but everyone else loved it as well. It was an exciting new idea, and novelty is a key component of motivating your staff.

My senior year, we didn't even make the playoffs. We didn't "Row the Boat" and it showed. Sadly, I never got to see the outcome of our year at that school. I was promoted to my current school after winter break and Covid then shut us down. I want to believe we would have reached our destination. We had plenty of people rowing toward it.

Dream Theme # 8: Row the Boat

EASE OF IMPLEMENTATION: Challenging. Finding oars, hanging items, placing names on little oars, getting keys and handing them out, and creating treasure boxes take time and effort. In a way, you have to "row" to make it happen.

RELEVANCE: Educators work their tails off. Many row boats daily. In some cases, the "runners" are managing multiple oars while rowing many boats and directing other vessels on the journey. This theme is perhaps the most relevant of all, thus far, given everything that we have going on in this profession.

MENTAL MEASURABILITY: Yes! Did they row the boat with their team or, when needed, alone, so that the group would be moving in the right direction?

EXAMPLES: Hard work pays off, and that basically is what the idea of rowing is. Further, teamwork pays off even more if everyone is in the same boat rowing with synergy. There are many stories out there of people who did amazing things just by hustling. Find someone that your staff can connect to and run with it!

PITFALLS: Minimal.

THE REVEAL: There are a ton of P.J. fleck videos and graphics available. As of 2023, he continues to work to "change their best" and "row the boat" and can often be seen making a rowing motion on the sidelines!

WHO / WHAT WILL GET BUY-IN TO THE IDEA? The oars and keys open up so many possibilities. And parents/communities want to give. If you hustle and share your vision, people love to recognize hard work!

Dream Theme 9: The Wild Card

"Failure is not an option!"

Gene Kranz

At the start of 2020, the world changed due to Covid. Coincidentally, many schools shut on Friday, the 13th. It was a tough time for the entire world, but in education, it was even more devastating. As I stated in chapter one, the year where I was opening up a brand new school (Tyrone Thompson ES in Las Vegas), doing so under the scrutiny and regulations that came along with the pandemic made the job even more difficult that it would have been under normal circumstances. It was a brand-new staff who hadn't hardly been able to be in the same room together, with a brand-new building that is extremely big, with brand new technology that may or may not work or even be an upgrade, with a brand new community of families who had never met us, and had no reason to trust us to with educating kids other than essentially blind faith.

Coming into that first meeting, I knew what the theme was, but it was going to be hard to reveal it or sell it online. Thankfully it could be adapted to the situation at hand. Again, we didn't know exactly what protocols were mandated due to constant changes, everyone was in masks, and it was undeniably difficult to try and build a team who would then go teach students online. With so much uncertainty, one movie came to mind!

In *Apollo 13*, the astronauts are flying to the moon, and it is Captain Jim Lovell's last mission in space. Everything is going well until a simple action causes a chain reaction for the history books. A manufacturing defect caused an explosion that left the spaceship crippled, but maneuverable. "Houston, we have a problem." was sent into the airwaves and a different mission began.

One scene that sets the stage for how Covid-19 affected education occurs as a crew of engineers have to design an air filtration system to cycle out the carbon dioxide that was accumulating in the cabin of the ship. If they did not succeed, the astronauts would surely have passed out and died. Finding a solution was mandatory, and in the end, you see a box of items dumped on to a table and they began building what was next to impossible.

In a way, teachers were essentially given the same task. Items were thrown onto their plate, and they had to organize it and then come through. If not, students would not have died, but their learning would have suffered even more than it did. The world handed educators this situation and they came through for kids and families as, so often, they do.

Going along with the idea that "failure was not an option" and we had to find a way to take a bunch of items and make them work when they were never supposed to be used in a certain way was the mission of the first year at the new school. However, it wasn't the content and the new materials or technology that concerned me as the leader, it was the attitude with which we went forth in the first year.

As I mentioned before, I attended the Ron Clark Academy in 2017 and found the environment next to none. During my visit, I also happened to meet Hope and Wade King who are the authors of "The Wild Card" which I listened to in the summer of 2018. Their book was well done, and I kept it in my mental file for the right time to utilize the contents. Two years later, it was a perfect fit.

The book discusses how you are essentially "The Wild Card" in your life, building, and classroom. You have to make the magic happen, regardless of what hand you are dealt in the moment. At that time in the world, we all needed to be "The Wild Card" and find a way to make the magic happen via distance learning, which was going to be a monumental task for all of us. Looking back, educators as a whole took a terrible hand dealt to them (Covid and Distance Learning) and won big (they made learning happen) despite the odds against them. They were "The Wild Card" in a time when they really needed to come through for all involved. When you throw in my situation with a new school, staff, community, etc., they were more than just a "Wild Card" – they were superheroes!

Starting out with the reveal, I played that scene described above from Apollo 13, which begins with Gene Kranz telling the men to, "find a way to fit a square peg into a round hole, rapidly." It then parallels our job that year where we are handed a mission as if it contained a bunch of spare parts and new items we have never used, but we had to come through. We then discussed the book by Hope and Wade King and how we had to go in with the right attitude and do the best you can with the ability and talent you have. Throughout the year, we did other fun things as able given the pandemic protocols, and we wrote "212" cards that were relabeled "Wild Cards" now. Every teacher received a giant playing card to hang in their room as a reminder to be that person that kids and families needed that year as well.

Using books, as you'll see with this chapter and the next few, are easy items to design a theme around. They can easily make you better in so many ways and, further, you never know where they will lead. In 2022, Hope and Wade King selected Tyrone Thompson as their national model for 'Rock Your School Day' which is a movement they began which highlights fun and engagement environments in educational settings. They visited our campus that day and brought national recognition to our campus, validating that we are definitely "Wild Cards" in our profession. Our school district, CCSD, also utilizes the same theme for new educators every year to inspire them to be great as well.

DREAM THEME # 9: THE WILD CARD

EASE OF IMPLEMENTATION: Very easy. Make a Power Point presentation discussing the points in the book, "The Wild Card" and then get creative. Create cards and have pictures with them. Do drawings as we did for prizes. Play a game with cards or decorate the building somehow with suits or the cards themselves. The possibilities are endless. I believe you can even book Hope and Wade King to speak at your school if you are all in.

RELEVANCE: Extremely relevant each year. People need to be go-getters every year, not just the year coming out of a pandemic. In everyday life, you hold "The Wild Card"and can make your hand what you need to win.

MENTAL MEASURABILITY: Many times a day. Are you making positive changes or keeping the hand you're dealt?

EXAMPLES: See Apollo 13. They were dealt a bad hand and figured it out. Who else do you know that has done that?

PITFALLS: Minimal.

THE REVEAL: So many ways. Use the clips and the book, buy some cards, play a game with them, such as a big giant game of war between grade levels and departments. Make it fun because you are a "Wild Card" also!

WHO / WHAT WILL GET BUY-IN TO THE IDEA? Everyone can! Parents can see when you go above and beyond. Maybe pass it down into your classroom where kids are "wild" and when they do something extraordinary they are rewarded. In the end, if you work to make things better, you are improving the hand you were dealt.

DREAM THEME 10: BE RELENTLESS

Coming off the year described in the last chapter, the common statement heard in education was "learning loss" and many educators felt that a majority of kids were behind in some way. There were plenty behind academically, to be sure, but those that were on grade level were more than likely behind socially now as well.

A friend and colleague of mine was selected to open a new middle school about two miles from where my school was located. She was "housed" at mine while planning until she could officially move into her new location. It was during that planning that she told me about a middle school principal who was covered with tattoos, rode a skateboard, and his school was decorated like graffiti. I was just about done with the decorations at my school, but I thought that was a neat idea given that kids probably were into that type of design. It wasn't going to fit anywhere in my building, but I continued to learn about the principal through her until I had to look into him myself. Once I did, I was hooked!

Hamish Brewer is a highly unconventional, yet extremely motivational kind of guy. His energy and dedication is top shelf and principals should definitely take lessons from him. It was after watching a few videos of him where he was featured in the news that I was hooked and his book *Relentless* was a perfect fit for what we needed. Many of our kids were "behind" yet they were back on campus, and we didn't have time to waste. We had to be relentless with our actions and get these kids back on track in every way. It was going to take a lot of energy to do it, passion was amplified, and it was truly "go time" for our profession.

Anyone who has visited Tyrone Thompson ES, or who works there, knows that the hallways are important. The environment is a high priority for me, as I want parents to hear their kids saying that they love the way the school is designed. During a meeting with the teacher who essentially planned and created almost all of the original decor and logos, we came up with a way to make it even more incredible through the painting and use of every hallway space. It was while I was finishing up painting the final hallway for the opening of the school year that I had a thought. How cool (and how much would it cost) to have Hamish Brewer come kick off our year and our theme? My colleague quickly did some research, and it wasn't necessarily cheap...and as I was standing on a ladder, I thought, "F it, why not?" Fast forward to the beginning of August and I was meeting the person who wrote the book that we were using to motivate the staff that year.

For the reveal, they had absolutely no clue in the world, which made it fun for some, nerve wracking for those who don't like surprises, and off the charts exciting for me!

Another colleague wanted in as well, and given that middle schools had gyms, we all collaborated and came up with a way to have them meet the first day back in that space with no clue what was to come. I sent out clips of Mr. Brewer the last few days of summer (it was their choice to watch or not) that were motivational, inspiring, and yet, they showed we didn't have time to waste. On their chairs when they arrived were t-shirts designed with "Be Relentless" in them, as well as the book, *Relentless* by Hamish himself. But then, when he walked out, that was fun! They had no idea what they were in for, and Hamish Brewer did not disappoint. By the time they left, it was set up to be a great year!

Once back at school, I still did a slideshow to cement the fact that we had to be relentless with these kids. They needed our best effort and we had to keep the momentum going that we had built at the end of the year in terms of building our school and our trust with the community.

As you may have noticed, from year one to year 10, the idea of themes has grown into a great act of excitement now. I thrive in it, and use it to give them a rallying point, a North Star so to speak, that we can row our boats toward. We also added shirts to the mix with the theme, which we wore every Monday to remind us of that mantra. We also added it to our first day for students, having specialists build it into the day and telling kids to be relentless with their actions as well. "212" aka "Wild" cards were now identifying those who were relentless in their pursuit to educate students. However, having Hamish come to start us off, and then taking it to where we went next year, proved that this work is important for a staff and a school to have as the year begins.

DREAM THEME # 10: BE RELENTLESS

EASE OF IMPLEMENTATION: Easy to hard to expensive. Guest speakers are not cheap, so that is a hurdle in many schools. Books are always good for some, but not all. In the end, it all comes down to how relentless you want to be with implementing this idea. Videos of Hamish are easily accessible, and you can make it yours.

RELEVANCE: Educators still must be relentless. We still do not have time to waste.

MENTAL MEASURABILITY: Daily. Did you do all you could to help as many as you could in some way?

EXAMPLES: Who is someone that just doesn't quit? Michael Jordan relentlessly went after being the best. J.K. Rowling and Dr. Seuss had to fight and scratch to get books published after being denied so many times. Examples are abundance depending on your audience.

PITFALLS: Depending on your level of relentlessness, minimal to some. Money can always be tricky, but there are plenty of positives to be found!

THE REVEAL: How far do you want to go?

WHO / WHAT WILL GET BUY-IN TO THE IDEA? If you see a pattern here, that's good. Get parents and kids into it!

DREAM THEME 11:
RELATIONSHIPS OVER EVERYTHING

Relationships before rigor,

Grace before grades,

Patience before programs,

Love before lessons."

Dr. Brad Johnson

As I have said earlier, I never know when something is going to happen that will take our school down a path I did not see coming. Things just happen out of the blue, but you have to be willing to see and comprehend them when they slap you in the face!

Hamish Brewer's book was a catalyst for our school holding book studies after school. Teachers who could attend did, and the school took care of the rest. We usually plan out the books for the year in advance which helps me steer the ship where I want it to go with respect to school climate, instruction, or data. Naturally though,

Relentless was the first one that we covered.

I know exactly where I was sitting, as probably ten teachers were involved in a discussion about the book. We were around four weeks in when that moment struck. A fabulous teacher at our school made the statement, "I just wish people could learn that relationships matter more than anything!" Wow! Yes! I knew right then where we were going for the next year after "Be Relentless", and it was barely September! But how could I top this year?

For some reason, I still have the first screenshot that I took of a quote from Dr. Brad Johnson. On 5/22/20, he tweeted, "Some of the best leaders in education never leave the classroom. And good admins embrace them and their expertise." As you will see, I have a nostalgic feeling about that picture and am glad I kept it. But if you follow Dr. Johnson, you will see that he is all about relationships. He is one of the few educational gurus who preach about taking care of people as people and students as humans long before worrying about academics. It is because of his stance in these critical areas that I knew I had to have him kick off our year that "Relationships Over Everything" was our theme.

Derived from the statement in book study that was covered earlier, in reality, there is not a truer statement out there. Rita Pierson is famous for the statement, "Kids don't learn from somebody they don't like!" While yes, most kids love discipline, what they really love is knowing that someone cares about them. My educational hero is Joe Clark, the famous principal portrayed by Morgan Freeman in the movie *Lean On Me*. He was tough, but they knew he cared about them and their future, and that is why you see so many students outside the jail at the end of the movie. But my favorite thing that he does, which I saw him do on *The Oprah Winfrey Show* a year later, was that no matter what he said or heard from the students, he always told them he believed in them.

Relationships OVER everything was crucial in our third year at Tyrone Thompson ES. Covid protocols were essentially gone, so now we could form a bond and build connections with other kids and colleagues to a much higher degree. Our community could come together to heal and lean on each other academically and socially within a school. We could hold school nights and functions without huge concern for one's safety the way it was during Covid. We could work to accept each other for our beliefs and feelings, our strengths, and weaknesses, and what we brought to the team.

I had known for months that Dr. Johnson was coming to the school to open the year, and only one other person did as well (the office manager who had to do the paperwork)! He was due at around 9:30, so I had timed a game for the staff that shaped our relationships within our "houses" at Thompson. During the summer, I had also had them take an "enneagram" assessment to find out which of the nine personalities they possessed and then grouped them in that outcome. This was the basis for "relationships" this year, as everyone learned in the first thirty minutes what each number of the enneagram meant and how people felt in certain situations. They even all received a binder clip with the nine enneagrams broken down and summarized so they could gather information about a colleague as they were working with them. Finally, I started to play a "Monday Mindset" podcast episode from Dr. Johnson...except about halfway through, I stopped and said, *"You know what? Rather than listen to this, let's just hear it directly from him. Ladies and gentlemen, Dr. Brad Johnson!"* Then enters another famous educator to kick off our year and get us pointed in the right direction.

His message is affirmational and inspiring to educators and puts them in the spotlight of positivity. He covers working as a team (like geese), how to deal with conflict, treating students as the smartest humans ever regardless of their level, and that we should have relationships before rigor, grace before grades, patience before programs, and love before lessons. In the end, I presented him with a gift and a bag. In the bag which he opened was a shirt that held our theme for the year of "Relationships OVER everything!" It was a fantastic ending to the presentation.

Dr. Johnson modeled relationships while he was at our school afterward as well. He stayed and signed every book (all staff received "Dear Teacher" as a welcome back gift with their theme shirt and he then joined me and two staff members for a tour of the school, which he seemed to love! It was near the end of our time together when I asked him about publishing books and he showed me grace by saying that when mine was done, he would try to help me get it published. After he left, I received a message that he had forgotten his keys. It was my turn to show grace, as I quickly got them in the mail and sent them to his house in Georgia. But the relationship didn't end there. In fact, that was just the beginning.

That year we had "Relationship" cards and drawings with prizes, but the outcomes were extraordinary. Further, people were moved into positions within the organization that they could really blossom and collaborate with in a positive way. Grade levels were able to grow close in areas, and the office staff worked to do monthly morale boosters and create a positive environment for all staff members to the highest degree possible. The community gave us a 97% approval rating in a district survey and families seemed to love their school. This theme (along with the results) proved that relationships really do matter more than anything.

Dr. Johnson and I continued to correspond throughout the year, as we wished each other well in our journeys, as well as always commented or liked social media posts. Yet, sometime around February, he sent me a message that basically asked me to partner with him to co-author a book about creating teams. Our relationship turned into a partnership and now is also a friendship. It was during dinner in the summer of 2023 that I asked him, "*I just have to know, why me? Why did you choose me?*"

He said, in his southern drawl, "I just liked the way you did things when I visited." As I said, you never know when things are going to take a turn down a different path.

DREAM THEME # 11: RELATIONSHIPS OVER EVERYTHING

EASE OF IMPLEMENTATION: Simple. The only trouble may be booking Dr. Johnson (or myself now) as he is busy headlining all over and I am still a principal. But we would love to come and discuss relationships or our new book! Even without us, you can always find a way to make relationships important.

RELEVANCE: See above. Relationships OVER everything.

MENTAL MEASURABILITY: Are you working to make things better for someone? Are you learning about a person as a person and trying to see their perspective with all items?

EXAMPLES: There are so many relationship examples. ESPN 30 for 30 highlights sports figures and you can use any of them to discuss relationships.

PITFALLS: Some people don't want to build them, or get over previous times they have been hurt by others. That has to be respected as long as they are respectful with their feelings as well.

THE REVEAL: Who / what will get "buy in" to the idea? Answer this question. Who can help you, or better yet, who can you help? Now get to know them and bring value to their life.

WHO / WHAT WILL GET BUY-IN TO THE IDEA? If you see a pattern here, that's good. Get parents and kids into it!

DREAM THEME 12: #LIVEYOURPURPOSE

Year 3 at Tyrone Thompson was a challenge on a personal level for me. There were so many positives, yet so many roadblocks to the path that I wanted to take the staff and school. It was a rollercoaster between district mandates, staff concerns, sickness, new staff members, and a growing school that had me questioning what the point of it all was. When I was selected to open the school, I did it with the intention of working to utilize the team and building to revolutionize education in some way. Many staff changes and a pandemic later, it wasn't going as planned and things just seemed to keep getting in the way.

Around October, not long after an amazing school dedication where we celebrated the life of Mr. Thompson with his family, I found myself up against the tide. It just seemed like we could not keep the momentum going and some did not want the momentum to happen at all. I walked across the parking lot, looked at the front of the school, and thought, "*What's the point?*" That is the moment that "purpose" became the next focal point.

When you hit the bottom of a dip, you have to find a way to pick yourself up. One of the #Thompson10+1 (ways to earn House Points) is "Conquering the Dip" and that was what we had to do. As many of the staff will tell you, I have a problem with planning for the next year too early. Most staff members do not want to talk about the next year in September of the current year! However, I believe that a leader is always looking forward to where the team needs to go, even as they are stuck in quicksand trying to get moving forward.

I am blessed to have an assistant principal (Shawna Quenneville) and strategist (Angie Brown) who get it. They see the need to plan and get as excited as I do when we discuss the future and the ideas we can implement with our next theme and kickoff for the school. Furthermore, it motivates them as well to help everyone get to where we need to be so that the theme next year works. And they saw my struggles and were with me through it all, so they understand exactly what I meant when I said #liveyourpurpose would be our next rallying point.

As I have said, I tend to have a memory bank for these types of ideas and am always thinking of items that can motivate a staff. This profession, in my opinion, requires leaders to motivate a group of people and lead from the front in order to get the most out of a group of adults. But you have to make it fun somehow! Not one educator wants to sit through a boring opening morning. Along with this belief, I have always wanted to do something completely unpredictable.

Nearly every adult enjoys bowling. The sport requires you to define your *purpose* every single time the ball goes down the lane. If you are the bowler, most of the time you are seeking a strike on the first toss, even when you are trying to be silly or do a crazy throw of some kind. With the second throw, your aim is to get a spare every time. There are no other options. That is your goal on the first and second throw. Even when you have a minimal chance of getting that pickup on the 7-10 split, you have hope and make your best effort and a focal point of where you are hoping to throw the ball. As a spectator, you have a purpose as well. You are cheering on your teammates, or rooting against them because they are close to beating you or you are chasing them. When you pay attention to their throw, you see if it is on line and if that throw serves your thoughts. It is a perfect metaphor for the idea of living your "purpose".

I originally had the thought that staff would show up the first day, walk the red carpet to cheers as they entered, and then come to the first staff meeting in the lunchroom ready to go. Then I thought about having everyone get up, walk outside, and get on a party bus that would take us to the bowling alley. The staff would have no idea where we were going, and the anticipation would be off the charts. We all go and bowl a game, and then we come back and springboard into our kickoff. Yet, when I thought about that, I had to consider that some staff members may not have liked that amount of unknown, and some had to bring their kids to school the first day, which I allow. In the end, we needed another idea.

Shawna, our assistant principal, then suggested that we could set the lunchroom up with a bunch of paint and easels and have it like a directed drawing activity. When you do those, you have a purpose to do the best you can, and it was a fun activity. The possibility was there, but the thought of all that paint and easels became quite expensive and time-consuming. Plus, we also thought that painting is difficult for many, and they needed to be able to be proud of their outcome.

In the end, we found a compromise for both! We organized the first "back to school" bowling night that occurred the Tuesday night before the staff returned. We had many members join and it was a fantastic time bowling and building relationships with our colleagues both old and new to the school. During the time at the bowling alley, Angie and I took videos of people bowling and we asked them prompts that led to the idea of "purpose" without using the word "purpose" such as, "What is your goal on this throw?" and "What are you trying to accomplish right now?"

The next morning, we started our year off with a video that Angie made of the time bowling which was a positive and fun beginning to our meeting. We then gave out a 14x18 white canvas that we separated into five specific sections (four quadrants and a circle in the middle). They also had Crayola markers. Then I led them through a slideshow that explained how we had gotten to where we are now.

In the end, they started by drawing anything that reminded them of bowling in the circle in the middle. In the top left quadrant, they drew or wrote what their goal for their school year was. In the top right quadrant, they did the same for their goals in their life. In the bottom left quadrant, they had to illustrate their plan for their careers. Finally, in the bottom right quadrant, everyone wrote #liveyourpurpose to remind them that their mission for the year was to do whatever they needed to make the three quadrants a reality. They, in a way, had a "purpose" for the year. Also, they could take that canvas and keep it wherever they needed to motivate and remind them of why they were at Tyrone Thompson at this point in time. Finally, every staff member received a T-shirt and an actual bowling pin with a tag on it that had our design for the year on. Three items, all tied together, and all that would remind them of their goals and the outcomes that they hoped to achieve. It was perhaps the most personal, powerful opening we have ever had, and in a time when educators are under fire, a reminder that what they do matters to many on a bigger level.

The new "212" cards also carried the t-shirt design and played off of the previous three years. They were "Living Their Purpose" by being the "Wild Card", "Being 'Relentless'", or putting "Relationships Over Everything" during the year. Further, every bowling pin and every "212 card" (now a "purpose" card) had a number. At the end of each semester, a drawing will be held for a group of prizes (donated gift cards or other items from businesses or parents) using these numbers, thus the more cards they receive, the better their odds of winning. We took it even further with our "house" system as well, having each house choose a charity to help this year giving them a "purpose" for working together to create a positive outcome. We also incorporated "purpose" into every staff development day as a way to bring them back to the bigger picture of what their lives and careers are for.

My own "purpose" this year is to help the staff and community in any way I can, putting them first and my needs at the end while leading from the front. Personally, I have been blessed to do a ton of what I had hoped in my life when I became a dad and have worked in a career that I have enjoyed in some way each day. But my future purpose includes my hopes of retiring and getting to know my grandchildren well. As for the rest of my career, I am working to revolutionize education in some way while hustling to put our school, Tyrone Thompson ES, on the map nationally as the model for what a public school can and should be. What is your "purpose" in those areas?

DREAM THEME # 12: #LIVEYOURPURPOSE

EASE OF IMPLEMENTATION: Simple.

RELEVANCE: Extremely. We all have "purpose" and want to have meaning with regards to what we do.

MENTAL MEASURABILITY: Daily. What are you doing to #liveyourpurpose?

EXAMPLES: Purpose is everywhere. But make it personal. Bowling with your staff is great for relationships and serves a "purpose" as well.

PITFALLS: Maybe a lack of drawing skills, but in the end, everyone can participate in their own way with this one.

THE REVEAL: Find something in your community that requires a focused "purpose" that your entire staff can do and wrap it around that. Maybe you all serve at a community center, or you all clean up a part of the city. Make it a positive or fun experience, yet relevant and meaningful as well.

WHO / WHAT WILL GET BUY-IN TO THE IDEA? We have "Houses" to utilize to create students and families to be a part of this. We also have centered a lot of our activities around the idea of "purpose" with respect to family nights and other items that involve our community.

DREAM THEME 13: TED TALKS

"Believe."

Ted Lasso

Looking forward, I know where I want to go with my school, but what about yours? What "dream theme" can you implement to get your staff moving in this type of direction? Where do you even begin? Why not with the most motivationally optimistic person in pop culture at this point in time: *Ted Lasso*!

The popular program featuring Jason Sudeikis was a smash hit and full of relevant and meaningful moments that can be related to a school. Ultimately, Ted is hired to do a job that he is not supposed to be successful at, yet his optimism and witty analogies find a way to turn around a culture that is toxic. While he knows nothing about soccer, he knows everything about building relationships, which is the subject of the first sentence in this book. Without relationships, you have nothing.

I came up with the unfounded belief that *Ted Lasso* was named that because he gives "Ted Talks" and can "Lasso" you into his way of seeing things in an outgoing and whimsical way. He has charm and charisma, but it is innocent at all times. There is something about a person who can find the positive in any situation and convey that positivity to a group of people. That approach can become infectious to the right group of people and the individuals who are allergic to positivity will quickly find a way to get out of the room.

Looking at using this program as a theme, I would invite everyone out to the field, give them jerseys, and play a game of soccer. Those that wanted to stand around can, those that want to cheer from the sidelines are allowed, and the competitors will go at it. Let's just have a friendly game of "football" as they say in England and hope nobody gets seriously injured. Serve drinks and snacks and maybe even invite the community to come and watch the staff have at it. Even more inclusive would be to have the staff somehow play students!

Once the game was over, and everyone caught their breath, we could then start a meeting by playing a clip or two of season one where you see a fractured group of people who cannot agree on much and show that star player (Jamie Tartt) being self-centered and egotistical. The viewers will easily see what is going on with the team, or lack thereof, and then they will reflect on where they are personally within that organization. You then discuss teamwork and your goals for the year and what you hope to accomplish, or have them accomplish as the months roll by, tying in your overarching theme, which could be many things with *Ted Lasso* at the helm. You could have the big idea of "teamwork", "optimism" or just "believe" and gear everything toward that. "212" cards can be adapted to any of those.

Take a moment to reflect on and answer this question. *"If I could get the staff to all see the importance of (insert answer), we would be so much better as a school".* If the answer is any of the three above, you can steer all conversations and actions toward that intended outcome. Then you simply find some clips that show the team and the ownership coming together as a family which leads to success in the end.

A final idea would be to give everyone a "believe" sign they can post in their room or wherever they need, as well to post "believe" throughout the building and on t-shirts, letterhead, memos, and everywhere else you can make relevant to the theme. Lastly, as you learn about the show, there comes a time when the "believe" sign gets torn up into pieces, only to be put back together when the team finally comes together. Give everyone a piece of the puzzle, number it, and have a raffle which requires them to have the piece to claim the prize. At the end of the year, when you have a luncheon to celebrate how much growth and change has occurred, have every team member bring their piece of the "believe" sign back and build a puzzle. After they leave, tape it together and hang in the lounge as a reminder of the year and the fact they should always "believe" in the process.

Lasso them in, just like Ted would.

DREAM THEME # 13: TED TALKS

EASE OF IMPLEMENTATION: Simple.

RELEVANCE: Adaptable and can be made to hit home in many areas of life

MENTAL MEASURABILITY: Daily. Do they still believe?

EXAMPLES: Tons of sports examples. You could easily blend in the 1980 USA hockey team and play parts of the movie, "Miracle on Ice" to show what a belief in a system and a team can do.

PITFALLS: Some people don't believe in a team. This is the chance for you to support those that do, the runners and joggers in your organization, and focus on moving that bus forward!

THE REVEAL: Play a soccer game – or have a watch party of a soccer game. Maybe even attend a soccer game!

WHO / WHAT WILL GET BUY-IN TO THE IDEA? Ideas to include the community are abundant. I listed a few, but you may have better ideas. Have the parents write notes to the kids during testing about how they believe in them. Or they can show their belief in the staff through their support. Believe in the process!

DREAM THEME 14:
#100POSITIVES

"The first thing we feed ourselves in the morning is our thoughts!"
  Dr. Brad Johnson

In my book, *It's All About Perspective*, there is a chapter in which I discuss the pros and cons of social media. I tell a story about a day in 2022, not long removed from the Covid days, in which there were many things going on at the start of the day, yet the counselor was off campus, and we were short staffed again. While usually very patient and able to just roll with the punches, this morning was different, and I made a calculated gamble. I was going to bring attention to the issue at hand, thus a post on social media was made.

While I believe and stand by what I said, the conversations that occurred after it, showed that in the end, it truly is all about perspective. The negative post led to much back and forth with people on "X" (Twitter at the time) and led to more conversations with powers that be. What it did not lead to was a change of the system, which taught me a valuable lesson, or at least what I have come to believe. No matter how negative you are, how much hell you raise on social media or to your supervisor, true change is made by leading from the front in a positive way. Negative posts get likes and conversation because haters love a chance to bring people down and bring themselves up. But when you lead with positives, they have a harder time poking holes in the joy. Further, although many may not admit it, everyone wants to work in a positive environment where happiness leads the way.

After internalizing the lesson above, the next required step is having a growth mindset and "conquering the dip" to overcome this adversity. While I admit that the counter action was part atonement, part animus, it was also one of the great changes I have made personally with regard to looking to the positive. That being stated, anyone that tells you, no matter how positive, that they don't have negative thoughts or make poorly chosen statements would be dishonest. We are all negative in some way, with some topics, but if we begin to try to find a positive perspective in all situations, we can slowly turn our mindset toward seeing beauty in all situations. Further, as a person who genuinely cares when they make mistakes or when they are criticized in some manner, I have to win my mental peace with results or changes that outweigh the action taken in the first place. The adage, "1000 positives multiplied by ONE negative equal one negative" is extremely personal to individuals like myself. Even with all of the good outcomes, anything that brings me down or is an energy vampire requires multiple moments of joy to combat the downer. It's a vicious cycle and mentally exhausting, but in a way, allows the positives to happen and be celebrated more. Remember, the bad times are what gets you from good time to good time.

At some point, a response from the negative post and subsequent interactions led to an idea. While I do not know where it stemmed from, it may be closely tied to the book *Dear Teacher* by Dr. Brad Johnson which highlights 100 aspirational stories for educators. Around the same time as the interaction online and with others described above, I was in the middle of planning a visit by Dr. Johnson and interacting with his book. The idea #100positives was born and over a year later, here we are. I also decided to try to get others to engage in the same concept in order to make it bigger than me or my school, because the entire profession could stand an injection of positivity!

Positives can be found anywhere in your day; negatives get more notoriety/clicks/news. We are not always positive regardless of what we show the world through various forums. Everyone has bad days and sometimes your "C" game is your "A" game. Sadly though, we are all hard-wired at this time to be critical of others and items we do not agree with. Also, keyboard warriors are ample in the world, making it so easy to criticize anyone without repercussion or consequence. I call it the "teeter-totter" syndrome, where people push themselves up by pushing others down at the same time. We have become a society that, in many respects, is selfish and self-fulfilling. Often, others give credit to themselves long before lifting others, that is what the #100positives is attempting to change in some small way.

In a study cited by Heathline.com, it was concluded that those who were optimistic had a significantly lower risk of dying from several major causes of death, and that overall, it led to a better quality of life. "Positive thinking isn't magic, and it won't make all of your problems disappear. What it will do is make problems seem more manageable and help you approach hardships in a more positive and productive way."

Imagine if we all took that research, combined it with the #100postives, and could turn the perspective of educators around in some way. We could work together to see the good, post those moments, and learn from each other so we can promote happiness and great things happening in schools every hour of every day. Our current state of affairs in education is not positive in many areas and metrics across the country. The latest results rank the United States of America 14th overall, and Nevada ranks 46th in the quality of schools. This shows a need for the perception to have a facelift. However, what those rankings do not show are so many activities that engage kids in excellent life lessons. Assessments do not measure the level of relationships that teachers have with students who have many hardships, trust issues, and show a lack of respect, yet one teacher finds a way to help that kid become a successful member of a classroom. It doesn't measure that student who was NOT suspended yet was a frequent flier who met with the principal often, gained trust of an authoritative figure, and turned around behaviors that ordinarily would disrupt the learning of others. The examples of non-assessment positives can go on and on, and through the posts described below and others added on throughout the country, we can show the change to those that cannot quantify it.

While I have not made this a school-wide theme, the idea of having everyone buy into posting 100 positives in the year is highly intriguing. I continue to complete this act and have dragged a few people into the hashtag hoping to get them to #25 positives, but this one takes dedication. People have to be committed and not interested in this one to make it to the end goal. However, imagine if every staff member found 100 positive thoughts and posted them somewhere. A staff of 75 would have around 7,500 posts that paint the school in a radiance unequaled by any other school on social media.

DREAM THEME # 14: 100 POSITIVES

EASE OF IMPLEMENTATION: Simple. It just requires individuals to see the positives which is more difficult, at times, than finding the negatives.

RELEVANCE: Entirely relevant to bringing positivity to the school. If someone has a negative culture, use this one to help turn it around.

MENTAL MEASURABILITY: Daily. If you cannot find something positive in the day, you should not be in the field of education.

EXAMPLES: Check out the @RobertH_2334 account on Twitter (X) and get plenty of ideas. Look on social media for anyone who has positives about their school or classroom or students. The possibilities are endless.

PITFALLS: Some people live in the negative and can only see issues with everything. There are people who can poke holes into heaven and if you gave them a million dollars, they would want it in small, non-denominational bills and add an extra dollar just because they said so.

THE REVEAL: Pick someone that you feel is the most positive person in the world and play a video of them, or find some motivational posts and run with it. Create a slideshow of the positives of your school and then require everyone to post a positive at that moment. Have some challenges about who can post the most by a certain date. Give them categories that they can post about and reward them somehow. There are so many ways to get them thinking in this way!

WHO / WHAT WILL GET BUY-IN TO THE IDEA? After you get the teachers rolling, bring in the kids and the community. Can they post 1000 combined positives about your school? If you have houses, which house can win? If you truly want to turn around the negativity, drown it out with the positive!

IN THE END

"Remember, in the end no matter where you stand on the issues, it's all about perspective!"

Robert Hinchliffe

In the event that you have a staff that is trying to come together as a team but just cannot, and you need to try to find a way to get them to work together, may I suggest the theme, "Perspective" to you?

I would be happy to come to your school and provide an inspirational kick-off to your school year. I have a presentation that I use when speaking that combines the book that I co-authored with Dr. Brad Johnson with my other book, *It's All About Perspective* and shows multiple ways of building a team while looking at different points of view. Through this interactive presentation that reaches people on various emotional levels, we can set you up to help the staff see items from all viewpoints, whether it be administration, colleagues, parents, or whoever else plays a part in your day-to-day operations. You can take the "V" principles from the book *Building Dynamic Teams in Schools* and create teams and a process for various actions within your school, such as adaptability, communication, collaboration, and using diversity as a strength. The presentation can be tailored to hit your main overarching theme that you want to instill in your staff.

The "V" principles are a way of completing the managerial tasks of a school in a way that creates a positive culture amongst the staff that buy into what we would be selling. You can use them to tackle any situation that may arise during the year where your team is struggling and in need of guidance on how to find the right outcome to the concern at the time. Also, by looking at all "perspectives" of the individuals involved, a better understanding and decision-making process can be completed leading to a higher level of successful outcomes. By the end of the presentation, your staff will be ready to collaborate and grow as a team with you at the helm leading from the front heading in the direction you wish to go.

In the event that you have a different idea, my two colleagues who are mentioned in the chapter about #livingyourpurpose (Shawna Quenneville and Angie Brown) are partnering with me to create a "Dream Themes" company where we will work with you to develop any theme that you wish to tackle. We can provide all digital media, slideshows, "212" card designs in conjunction with t-shirt designs, building upgrades or remodels of the lounge, and will collaborate with you to "make your 'dream theme' come true!"

My perspective is that themes work. They bring a community of educators together for one common overarching goal, and we can work together to create the kind of environment that you wish to work in. Throughout my years as a principal using them to enhance a school climate, or as a spectator watching various teams or organizations use them for a common purpose, I "believe" that they can make a difference in a school which equals a better educational experience for children within those buildings. Whether or not you run with them yourself or with a colleague, or you contact me directly to have our team assist you in building the kind of culture you want in this area, I hope all of your "themes" come true. Regardless, in the end, no matter where you stand on the idea of themes, it's all about perspective.

.

LET US HELP YOU CREATE YOUR "DREAM THEME" FOR THE UPCOMING YEAR!

Angie Brown, Shawna Quenneville, and Robert Hinchliffe are all educators at Tyrone Thompson Elementary School in Las Vegas who have a passion for inspiring teachers. They will work with you to create not only your theme, but a presentation, morale boosters, T-shirts, and anything that you wish to have to take your school environment to another level.

Contact us to start planning your "Dream Theme" today.

We look forward to working with you!

FOR MORE INFO, PLEASE EMAIL US AT:

educationaldreamthemes@gmail.com

Works Cited

Apollo 13. Directed by Ron Howard, Universal Pictures, 1995.

Clark, Ron. *Move Your Bus: An Extraordinary New Approach to Accelerating Success in Work and Lif.* Simon & Schuster Audio, 2015.

Friday Night Lights. 2006.

Gleason. Directed by J. Clay Tweel, Amazon MGM Studios, Open Road Films, 2016.

Johnson, Brad, and Hal Bowman. *Dear Teacher.* Routledge, 2021.

Johnson, Brad and Hal Bowman. *Relationships Before Rigor, Grace Before Grades, Patience Before Programs, Love Before Lessons.* Routledge, 2021.

King, Wade, and Hope King. *The Wild Card: 7 Steps to an Educator's Creative Breakthrough.* 2018.

Krantz, Gene. *Failure Is Not an Option: Mission Control From Mercury to Apollo 13 and Beyond.* 2009.

Lean On Me. Directed by John G. Avildsen, Warner Bros., Warner Bros. Pictures, 1989.

Parker, S. L. *212 the Extra Degree: How to Achieve Results Beyond Your Wildest Expectations.* 2022.

Perna, Mark C. "Why Organizations Need a Rally Point." *Medium,* 22 May 2018, https://medium.com/@MarkPerna/why-organizations-need-a-rally-point-608bf617fcfa.

Ted Lasso. Directed by Declan Lowney, 2020.

The Guardian. Directed by Andrew Davis, Touchstone Pictures, Walt Disney Studios Motion Pictures, 2006.

About the Author

Robert Hinchliffe is a successful principal in Las Vegas, Nevada, and has been an administrator for over 18 years. His unique experiences in various schools allow him to give input into areas that challenge educators on a daily basis. His career accomplishments include leading various 5-star rated schools, schools that have received distinguished awards, and he was selected to open Tyrone Thompson Elementary School in 2020. His daily goal is to run one of the most exciting and stimulating school environments in the country and continue to lead "the model of what a public school can and should be" while fighting against the status quo. He has seen many changes and situations that have shaped his perspectives on topics in the field of education. He is the author of the book, "Building Dynamic Teamwork in Schools" with Dr. Brad Johnson and also authored "It's All About Perspective" while hosting a podcast with the same name. He spends most of his spare time with his wife as they navigate the many activities of their five daughters but is always able to find time to discuss educational topics with anyone willing to listen.